You Can't Make a Move Without Your Muscles

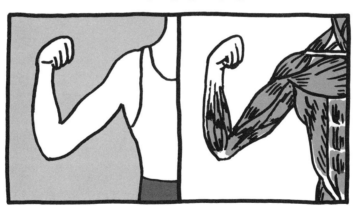

D0845665

PAUL SHOWERS

You Can't Make a Move Without Your Muscles

Illustrated by Harriett Barton

Thomas Y. Crowell   New York

OTHER *Let's-Read-and-Find-Out Science Books* BY PAUL SHOWERS

A Baby Starts to Grow · *Before You Were a Baby* (with Kay Sperry Showers) · *A Drop of Blood* · *Hear Your Heart* · *How Many Teeth?* · *How You Talk* · *Look at Your Eyes* · *Me and My Family Tree* · *No Measles, No Mumps for Me* · *Use Your Brain* · *Your Skin and Mine*

Let's-Read-and-Find-Out Science Books are edited by Dr. Roma Gans, Professor Emeritus of Childhood Education, Teachers College, Columbia University, and Dr. Franklyn M. Branley, Astronomer Emeritus and former Chairman of The American Museum-Hayden Planetarium. For a complete catalog of *Let's-Read-and-Find-Out Science Books*, write to Thomas Y. Crowell, Department 363, 10 East 53rd Street, New York, New York 10022.

Text copyright © 1982 by Paul Showers   Illustrations copyright © 1982 by Harriett Barton

Library of Congress Cataloging in Publication Data
Showers, Paul.   You can't make a move without your muscles.
Summary: Introduces the muscles of the human body and describes
how they enable the parts of the body to move.
1. Muscles—Juvenile literature. [1. Muscles. 2. Motor Learning] I. Barton, Harriett, ill. II. Title.
QP321.S47 1982 612'.74 81-43323 ISBN 0-690-04184-5 AACR2 ISBN 0-690-04185-3 (lib. bdg.)
1 2 3 4 5 6 7 8 9 10

You Can't Make a Move Without Your Muscles

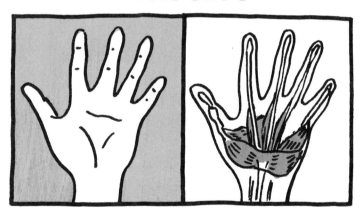

STOP!

Before you do another thing:

1. Make a funny face.
2. Hop up and down on one foot five times.
3. Scratch your head with one hand and pat your stomach with the other.

Now, turn the page.

When you made a funny face, you used muscles in your cheeks. You used muscles in your legs when you hopped up and down. You used muscles in your hands and arms when you scratched your head and patted your stomach and when you turned the page.

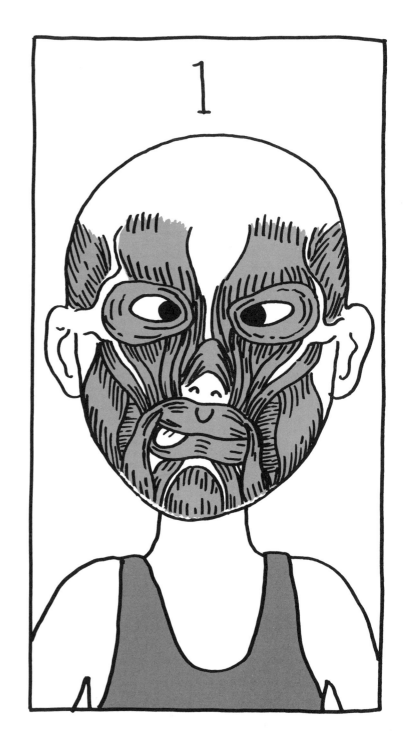

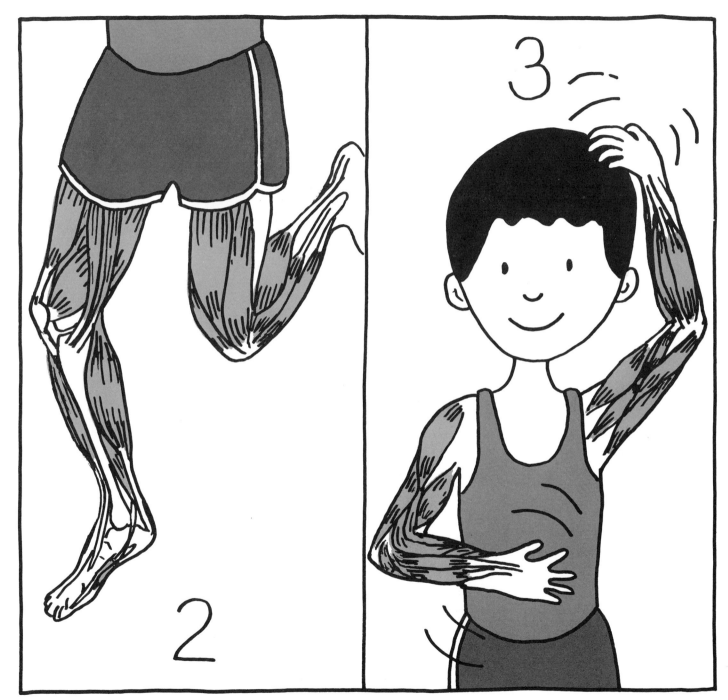

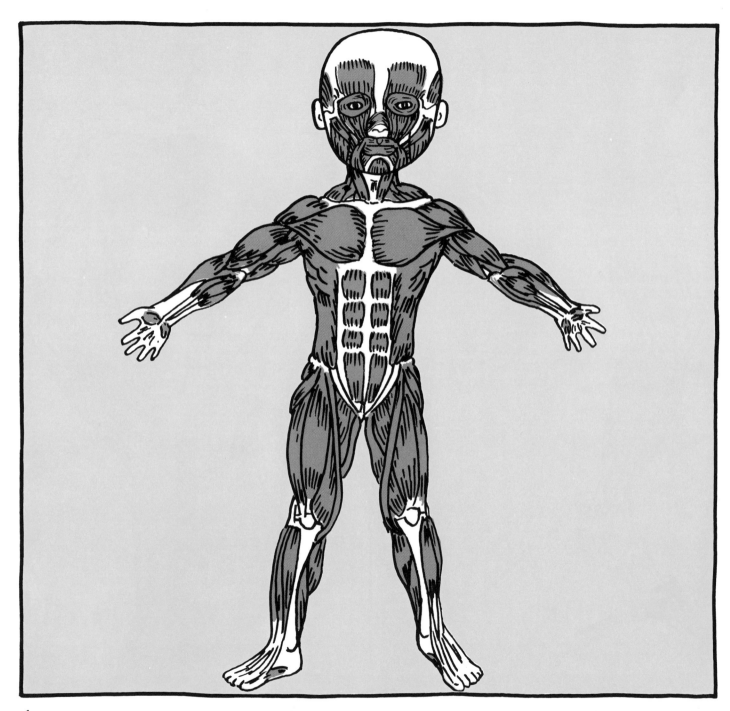

Every time you move any part of you, you use your muscles.

You even use muscles when you read.

There are more than 600 muscles in your body. Some are deep inside. Others lie just under your skin. Some are big and some are very small.

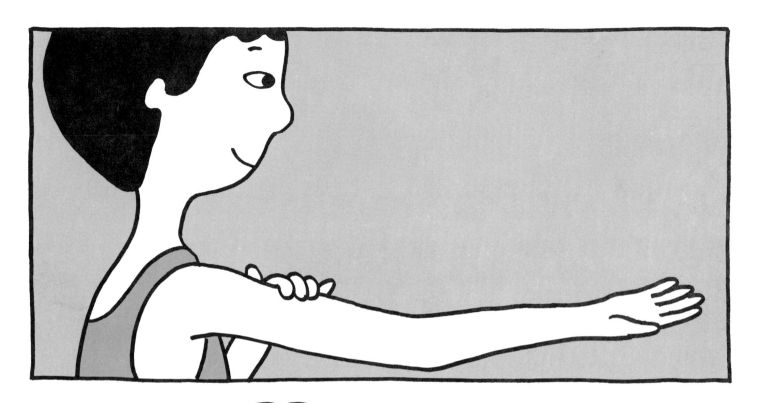

TRY THIS

Hold your arm straight out in front of you with the palm of your hand facing up. With your other hand, feel the upper part of your arm, the part between your elbow and your shoulder. You can feel a muscle there.

Make a fist with your right hand. Bring your fist up to your shoulder. You can feel the muscle in your upper arm change. It bunches up and gets harder. This muscle is called the biceps.

The top end of your biceps is fastened to a bone in your shoulder. The other end is fastened to a bone in your lower arm just below your elbow. When your biceps bunches up and gets hard, we say it is contracting. It is drawing itself together. When it does this, it pulls on your lower arm, your elbow bends, and your fist comes up to your shoulder.

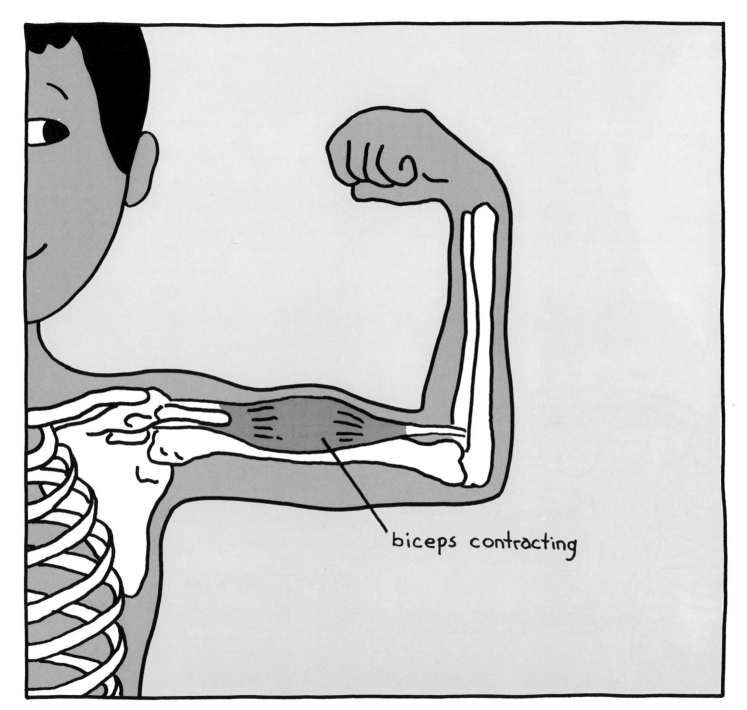

biceps contracting

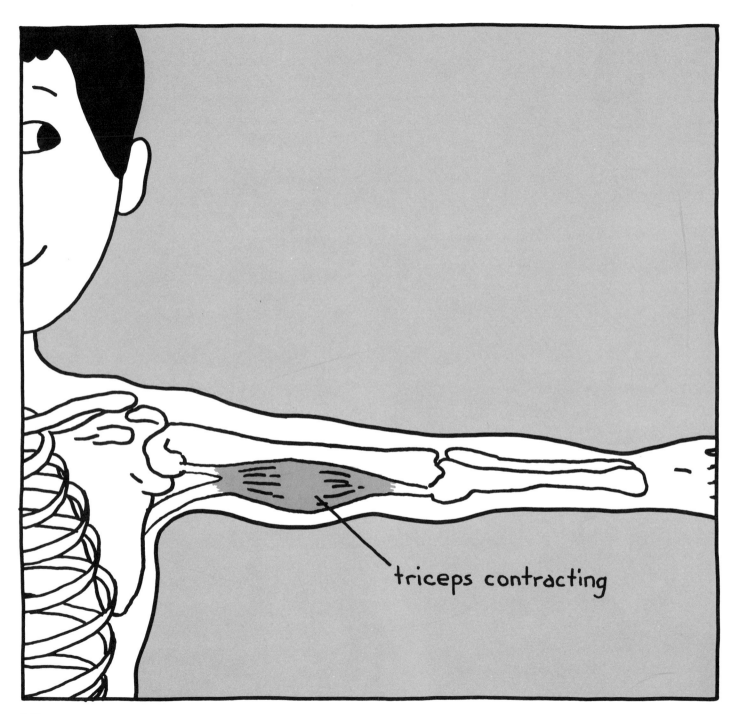

triceps contracting

Your biceps pulls your fist up to your shoulder. When you want to unbend your arm, you use another muscle. It is called the triceps.

Your triceps is on the back side of your upper arm. It also reaches from your shoulder bone down to a bone in your lower arm, just below the elbow. When your triceps contracts, it pulls your arm out straight again.

Your biceps and your triceps work together. First one pulls, then the other. Many other muscles in your body work in pairs that way. They pull back and forth.

By using your muscles you can turn and twist your arms and wrists. By using your muscles, you can bend over and stand up straight, and do a lot of other things.

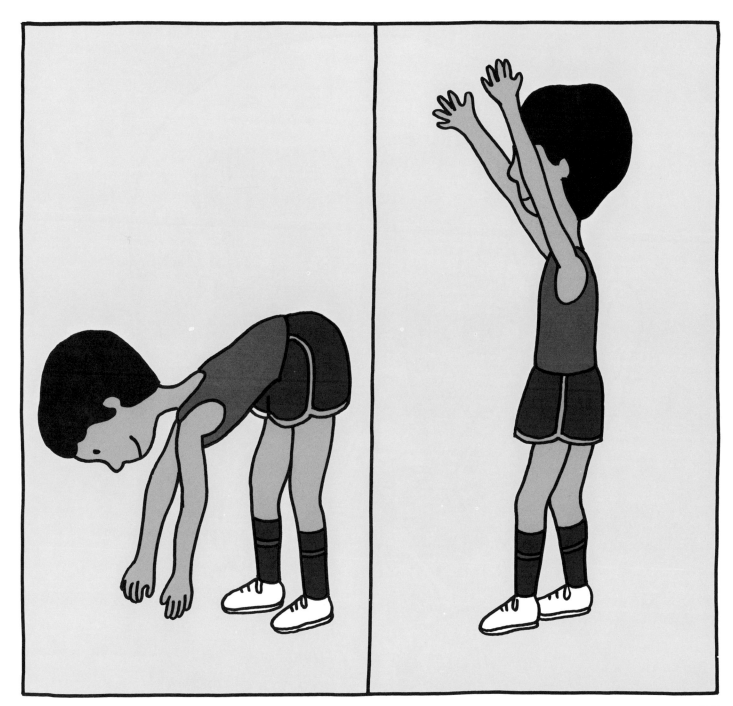

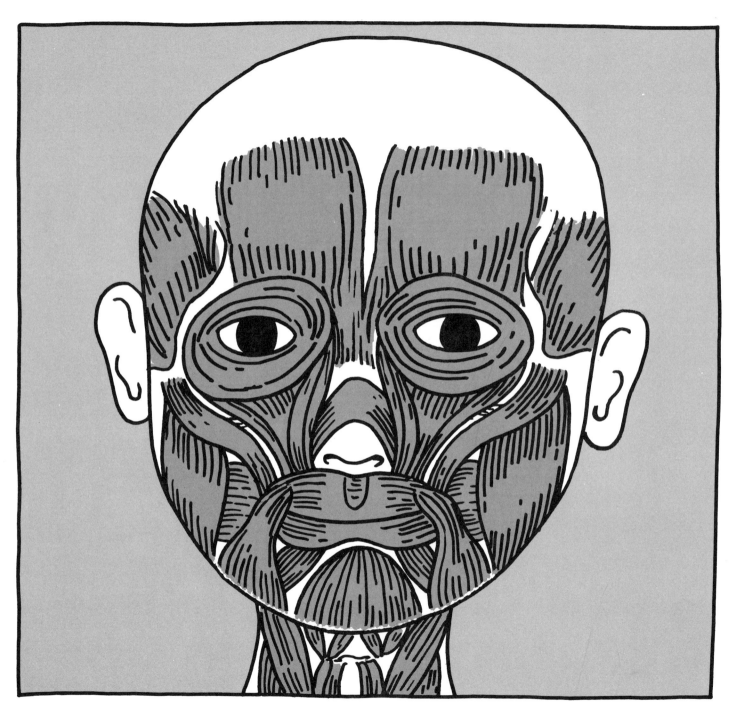

14

Many of your muscles are fastened to the bones of your skeleton. They are called skeletal muscles.

Skeletal muscles are fastened to the bones in your face. You use them when you open and close your mouth. You use them when you smile and frown and wiggle your nose.

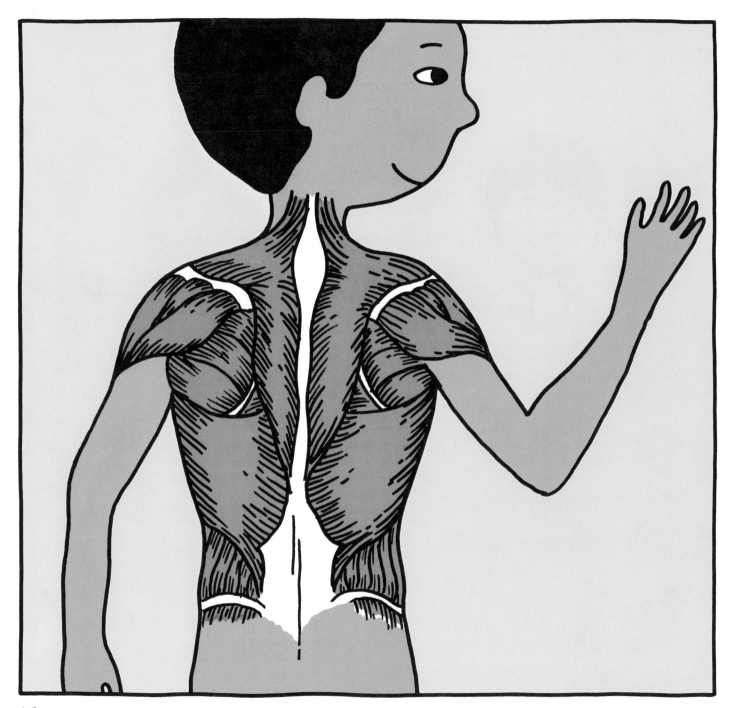

You have skeletal muscles
in your back. You use
them when you move your
neck, shoulders, arms, and back.

You have skeletal muscles
in your legs. Some reach
from your hip bones down to
your knee bones. Others
reach from your knees down
to your feet.

They all work together
when you walk, run, jump,
or kick.

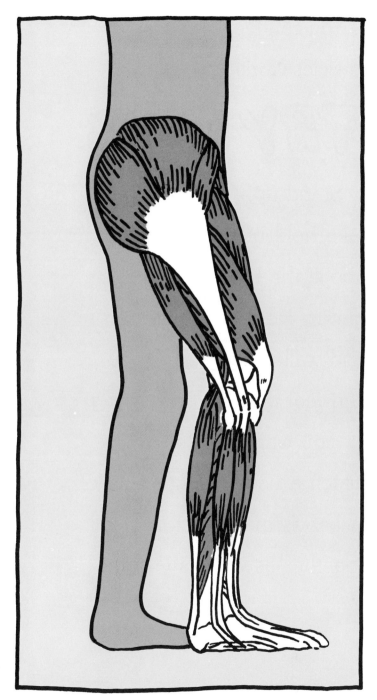

You can feel your leg muscles working.

TRY THIS

Stand up. Bend over and take hold of your left leg above the knee. Use both hands. Hold onto your leg and walk a few steps. You can feel the muscles pulling as you walk. Did you ever watch a baby trying to walk? A baby's muscles don't work together as well as yours.

19

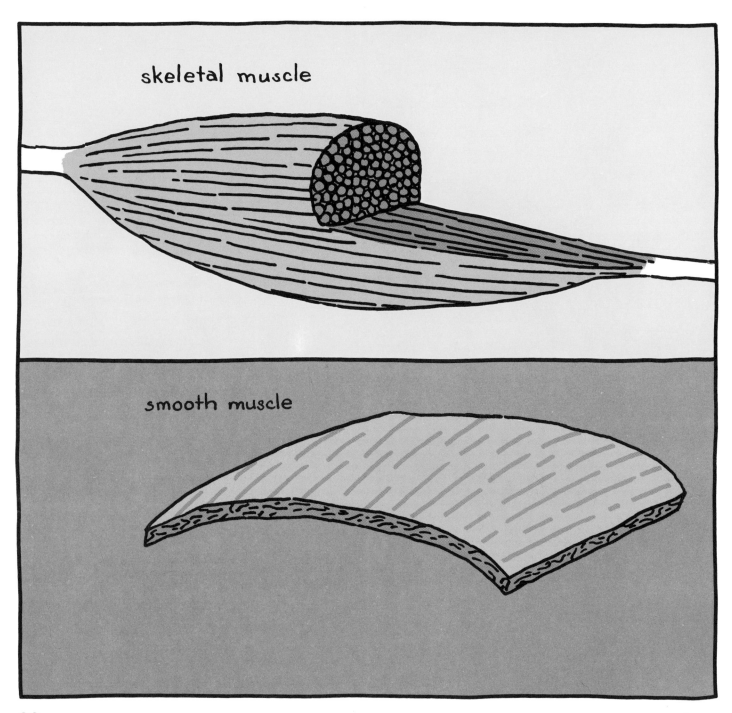

skeletal muscle

smooth muscle

You have another kind of muscle in your body. These are called smooth muscles. Both skeletal muscles and smooth muscles are made of long, thin fibers. In skeletal muscles, the fibers lie side by side in thick bundles. In smooth muscles, the fibers are spread out in sheets.

There are layers of smooth muscles in your throat. They help you swallow your food. Other smooth muscles are in your stomach and your intestines. They help you digest your food.

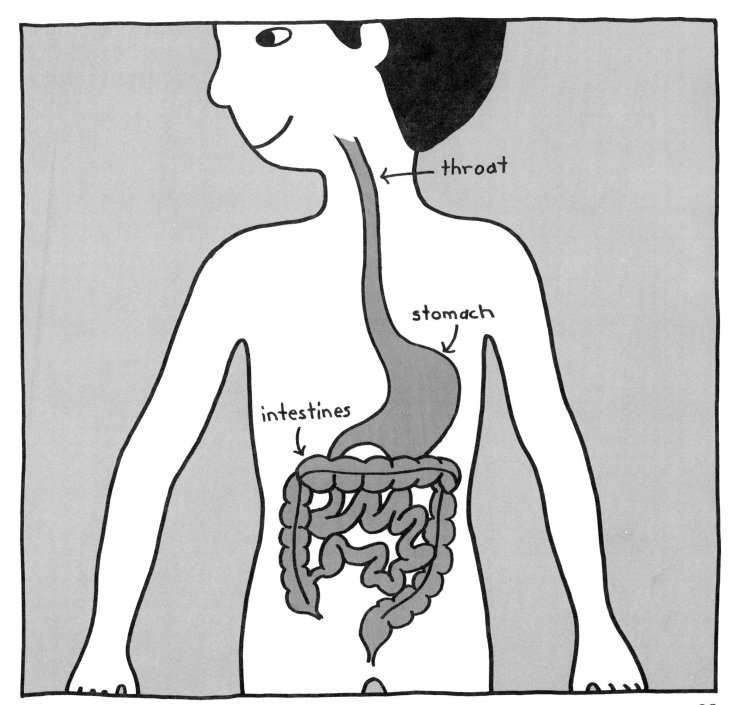

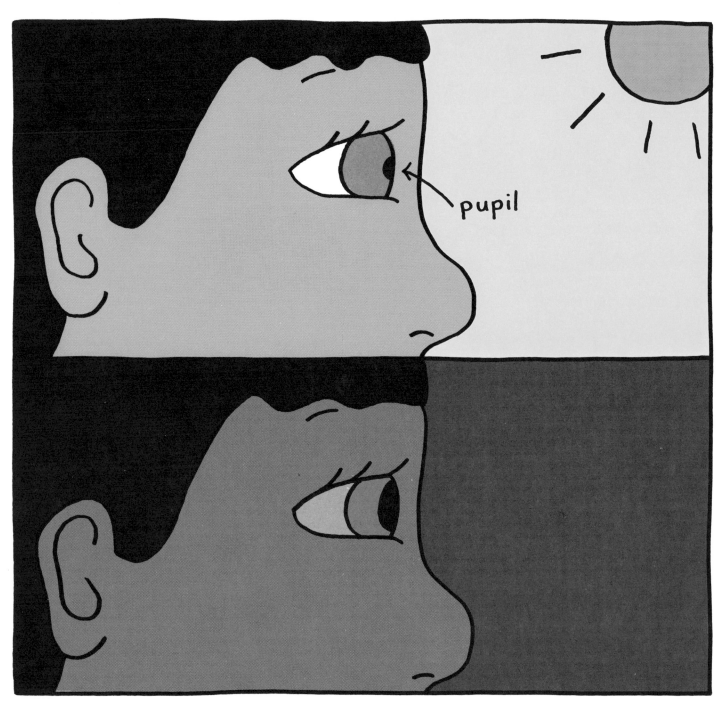

pupil

Small smooth muscles change the size of the pupil in your eye. They pull the pupil open when your eye needs more light. They make the pupil smaller when there is too much light.

Your heart is a special kind of muscle. It is the only muscle of its kind in your body. It works all the time, even when you are asleep. All day and all night your heart keeps pumping blood through your body. It pumps hundreds and hundreds of gallons of blood a day.

If your heart and your smooth muscles are healthy, they never get tired. That makes them different from skeletal muscles. When skeletal muscles work hard, they do get tired. Then they need to rest. But not for long. All muscles must work to stay strong.

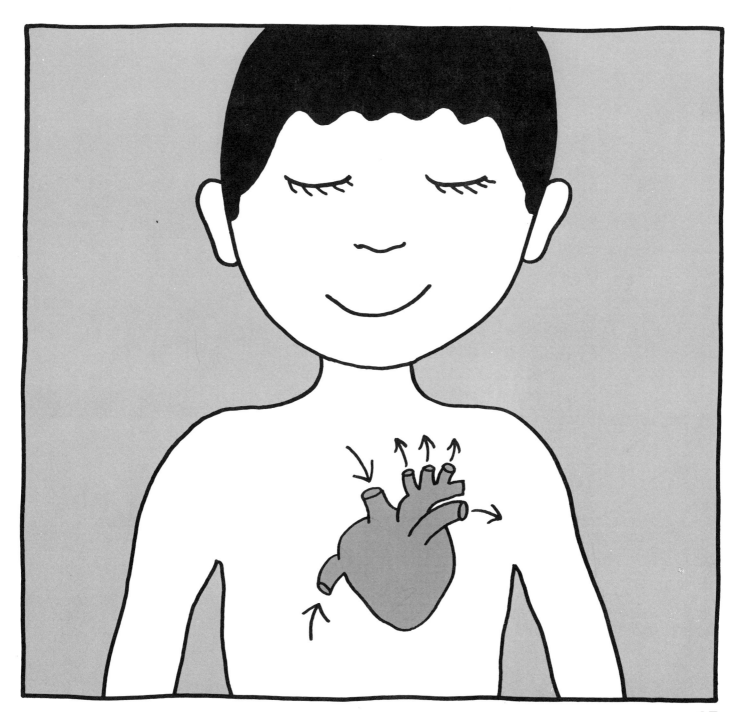

If you break a leg, your bones will need a rest so they can heal. A doctor will put your leg in a cast. You won't be able to move the muscles in your leg for six weeks or more. When the doctor takes off the cast, you'll be lame. The muscles in your leg will have rested too long. They will be weak. It will be hard for you to walk.

But the doctor will tell you to do special exercises. And before you know it, the muscles in your leg will be strong again.

Walking and running are good exercise for your muscles. Turning somersaults is good for your muscles, too. So are swimming and roller-skating and bike riding.

31

Because you have strong muscles, you can climb stairs. You can bat and catch a ball and jump rope. You can lift a heavy pail of water.

Muscles are very important. You can't make a move without them.

About the Author

Paul Showers is a retired newspaperman and the author of nearly two dozen books for children. He first became interested in writing for young readers after having watched his own children struggle with the "See, Sally, see" books of the 1950s. His own works—most of them in the Let's-Read-and-Find-Out series—consistently reflect his belief that children's books can be both lively and worthwhile.

Mr. Showers has worked on the Detroit *Free Press*, the New York *Herald Tribune*, the New York *Sunday Mirror*, and for twenty-nine years, on the Sunday *New York Times*. He was born in Sunnyside, Washington, and was graduated from the University of Michigan, where he received an A.B. degree.

About the Illustrator

Harriett Barton was born in Picher, Oklahoma, and grew up in nearby Miami. A graduate of the University of Kansas, she presently lives in New York City, where she works as a designer of children's books. She has illustrated a number of children's books, including *Cactus In The Desert* and *No Measles, No Mumps For Me*.